BATS

SCHOLASTIC INC.

New York   Toronto   London   Auckland   Sydney
Mexico City   New Delhi   Hong Kong   Buenos Aires

Written by Kris Hirschmann.

Cover illustrations by Mick McGinty and Carolyn Bracken.
Interior illustrations by Carisa Swenson, Ted Enik, and Carolyn Bracken.

Based on *The Magic School Bus* books
written by Joanna Cole and illustrated by Bruce Degen.

This book is a nonfiction companion
to *The Magic School Bus: The Truth about Bats.*

The author would like to thank Jacqueline J. Belwood, Ph.D., Scientist in
Residence at the Cincinnati Nature Center, for her expert advice
in preparing this manuscript.

ISBN 0-439-31435-6

12 11 10 9 8 7 6   2 3 4 5 6 7/0

Cover designed by Carisa Swenson.
Interior designed by Madalina Stefan.

Printed in the U.S.A.   40

First Scholastic revised printing, October 2002

Contents

A Note from Ms. Frizzle

Dear Readers,

Before I board the Magic School Bus, I always try to learn as much as I can about our field trip topic. It was no exception when we set out to discover <u>The Truth about Bats</u>.

Of course, I have to give my class a lot of credit. They discovered many wonderful things about bats, too.

I'm excited to share the class notes from our bat unit with you. You can use the facts you find here in a report of your own.

Happy fact-finding,

Ms. Frizzle

BATS

Who knew there was so much to learn about bats?

BIG BOOK OF BATS

Chapter 1

What Makes a Bat a Bat?

What's that thing flittering around in the evening sky? It could be a bird that hasn't returned to its nest for the night. But chances are the creature you see is a bat.

When the sun goes down, bats wake up. They leave their daytime hiding places and fly through the dark skies in search of food and water. People don't see very well in the dark, so we often don't notice bats. But on any warm night, there's a good chance they are around.

Is a Bat a Bird?

Some people believe that bats are a type of bird, but they're not. Bats are mammals, just like humans. But it's easy to see why people might get confused, because bats are the only mammals that can fly.

> A mammal is an animal that has fur. It also gives birth to live babies and nurses them with milk.

There are many important differences between bats and birds. One of these differences is easy to spot: Birds have feathers, while bats have fur. Other differences are harder to see, because they are internal (inside the body). For instance, birds have hollow bones that are especially light, which help them fly. Bats, however, have very thin bones that are filled with marrow (a soft, spongy tissue).

The bone structure of a bird's wing is also very different from a bat's. A bird's wing is supported by long, strong arm bones. There are finger bones inside each wing, but they are small and not very useful. A bat, on the other hand, has shorter arm

bones than a bird, but it has extremely long and delicate fingers. These finger bones spread out to support the wing membranes. (The membrane is the thin skin that covers the wing.)

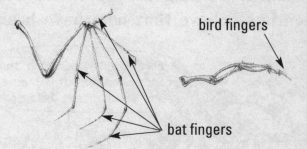

bird fingers

bat fingers

Another big difference between bats and birds is that bats, like most mammals, give birth to live young. Birds lay eggs that must be protected until the babies hatch.

Bat Evolution

Some people say bats look like rats or mice with wings. But bats are not flying rodents any more than they are birds.

Scientists have learned a lot about bats and their ancestors by

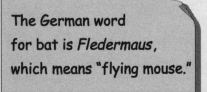

The German word for bat is *Fledermaus*, which means "flying mouse."

studying bat fossils. The oldest bat fossils that have been discovered so far are about 60 million years old, but scientists believe that bats have been

According to my research, the French word for bat is *chauve-souris*, which means "bald mouse."

around even longer than that —
perhaps as long as 100 million years.

No one is sure exactly how bats
evolved. The most popular theory is that
bats started out as gliding mammals.
Over millions of years, their bodies
continually changed until they were
able to actually fly.

Flying Anatomy

Bats fly by flapping their wings.
These wings are made of two layers of

Gliding Mammals

Although bats are the
only flying mammals, there
are a few other mammals
that can glide! Flying lemurs,
flying squirrels, and marsupial
sugar gliders have flaps of
skin along the sides of their
bodies that act like parachutes.

Some of these animals can soar up to 100 feet
before gravity forces them to land.

tough skin, or *membranes,* that enclose blood vessels (veins and arteries), nerves, muscles, and tendons (tissues that attach muscles to bones). The bat's arm and hand bones are also covered by these layers of skin. A tiny thumb, which the bat uses mostly for gripping and climbing, sticks out of the top of each wing.

Bats' wings are fragile and break easily. Even though wing membranes are strong, they are only about as thick as a plastic sandwich bag!

Without their wings, many bats really would look like mice. Most bats have furry bodies, small eyes, and perky ears. They also have two short back legs with clawed feet. Some bats even have mouselike tails! Some kinds of bats have tails that hang free. Other bats' tails may be partly or entirely covered by the tail membrane.

Bats come in many different sizes. Some really big bats have wingspans greater than 6 feet (1.8 m), while the tiniest bats have wingspans of less than 6 inches (15 cm).

Creatures of the Night

Bats are *nocturnal* creatures. This means that they are active mostly at night.

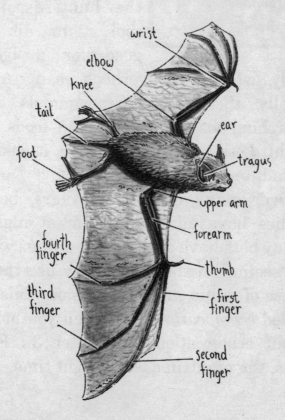

A bat's nighttime lifestyle has many advantages. For one thing, there are fewer *predators* (animals that hunt other animals for food) around at night. This helps to keep bats safe as they hunt. Also, the cool night air is good for a bat's body, which can overheat easily. And finally, there are fewer animals out searching for a bat's favorite foods at night. Less competition makes it easier for a hungry bat to fill its belly.

Owls and some snakes are nocturnal, too. Bats have to watch out for these predators!

Over many millions of years, bats' bodies have adapted to life at night. Many bats have developed a unique way of "seeing" in the dark. They use their sense of sound instead of vision. This is called *echolocation*. (We'll tell you more about echolocation in chapter 3.) For bats, the nighttime is the right time.

Mexican Free-tailed Bat

• **Just the Facts** •

Suborder: Microchiroptera

Body: 2.5 inches (6.3 cm)

Wingspan: 14 inches (35.6 cm)

Color: Dark gray to dark brown fur; black ears and nose

Location: Southwestern United States through Mexico to northern Argentina and Chile

Roost: Caves, rocky crevices

Food: Mostly small moths

During the daytime, thousands (sometimes millions) of these bats roost together in dark, damp caves. But when evening arrives, the bats become alert. They drop headfirst from their resting places and fly out of the cave in a long black stream. The departing bats look like a dark cloud that rises high into the sky and can be seen for miles around.

More than 20 million Mexican free-tailed bats roost in Bracken Cave near San Antonio, Texas, during the summer months. Another 300,000 make their home in New Mexico's Carlsbad Caverns.

As dusk falls near Bracken Cave, Mexican free-tailed bats fill the sky.

Bats live all over the world.

Chapter 2
Types of Bats

There are about 4,500 different *species* of mammals in the world. (Species is a word scientists use for different kinds of plants and animals that share the same traits.) Bats currently account for 950 *species* of mammals. And scientists believe that there are many kinds of bats that haven't been discovered yet, so no one knows how many species of bats there really are!

There are almost 1,800 different species of rodents in the world. There are more rodents than any other kind of mammal. But bats come in second.

11

Megabats and Microbats

Scientists sort all living creatures into categories to make them easier to identify. The biggest category is called a *kingdom.* All animals — including humans — belong to the kingdom *Animalia.* After kingdoms come *phyla* (singular: *phylum*), *classes, orders,* and *suborders.*

Scientists who sort living things (animals, plants, bacteria, etc.) into categories are called taxonomists.

All bats belong to the scientific order Chiroptera (which means "hand-wing" in Greek). Within the Chiroptera, there are two suborders: the Megachiroptera (called megabats for short) and the Microchiroptera (microbats).

Bat classification:

Kingdom: Animalia (this includes all animals)

Phylum: Chordata (this includes all animals with backbones)

Class: Mammalia (this includes all mammals)

Order: Chiroptera (this includes all bats)

Suborders: Megachiroptera (megabats) and Microchiroptera (microbats)

"Mega" means big.

"Micro" means small.

■ Where megabats live

Megabats

There are about 175 different types of megabats in the world. They live only in the warm, tropical areas of Asia, Africa, Australia, and the Pacific Islands. Megabats feed on fruit and flowers, and they tend to be quite large, with wingspans up to 6 feet (1.8 m). Megabats have been nicknamed flying foxes because of their foxlike faces and large eyes.

Microbats

There are around 775 microbat species. Microbats can be found on every continent except Antarctica. They can live in warm or cool environments as long as there is ample food (mainly insects) and a place to roost. Microbats are usually smaller than megabats. Some microbats look similar to megabats, but others have much smaller eyes and longer ears.

Dinnertime

One of the major differences between megabats and microbats is what they eat. Megabats eat only fruit, *nectar* (the sweet liquid found inside flowers), and *pollen* (the powdery substance found

Frugivore is the scientific word for "fruit eater." *Carnivore* is the word for "meat eater." *Insectivore* is the word for "insect eater."

You're an insectivore, too, Liz!

in some flowers). In fact, megabats are also called Old World fruit bats because of their eating habits. Microbats also eat fruit and flowers, but they don't stop there. Different types of microbats eat flying insects, crawling insects, frogs, fish, lizards, small rodents, other bats, and even blood!

Bats with different diets use different

hunting techniques. Microbats usually depend on echolocation to locate their fast-moving food. Megabats rely mostly on smell and vision to find their meals. Most megabats do not echolocate at all.

Funny Faces

Sometimes you can guess how a bat hunts and what it eats just by looking at its head.

Megabats tend to have big eyes that help them to find fruit and flowers in the dark. Since they don't rely mainly on their hearing, their ears are usually small. Their noses are long and pointed. Many microbats that eat fruit and nectar also share these characteristics.

a megabat

Microbats that hunt for insects and animals depend mostly on their hearing, and not so much on their vision. Therefore they have small eyes and can have gigantic ears. They also have a flap of skin called a *tragus* inside each ear, and their noses may be flattened or oddly shaped. All of these features help them hunt using echolocation. (Find out more in chapter 3.)

a microbat

Some kinds of megabats hunt at dawn and dusk. This is probably because they use vision to find food, and they don't see very well in the dark. It is easier for these bats to find food when there is some daylight.

Microbats would rather hunt in the dark or near dark. Most of them don't depend on eyesight anyway, so they don't need light.

A bat's teeth also provide a good clue to its diet. Different kinds of bats can have teeth that are shaped and arranged differently—depending on what the bat eats.

Common vampire bat

American fruit bat

- Insect-eating bats have strong, sharp teeth with lots of ridges. The different shapes help grind and crush their food.

- Fruit bats often have simple peglike teeth for biting soft fruit.
- Some nectar-sipping bats, which feed by sticking out their long tongues, are missing their front lower teeth altogether. The gap in their teeth makes it easier to stick out their tongues.

> Some nectar-eating bats have tongues a third as long as their bodies!

- And vampire bats, which feed on blood, have two sharp front teeth that they use to nick their prey and make it bleed. They then lap up the blood. The rest of their teeth are almost useless.

It's All Relative

Even though megabats and microbats have important differences, they are alike in most ways. They have the same basic bone structure and body shape. They all fly. They have similar skin, fur, and habits.

When you get right down to it, a bat is a bat is a bat!

Lesser Long-nosed Bat

• **Just the Facts** •

Suborder:	Microchiroptera
Body:	3.5 inches (8.9 cm)
Wingspan:	14–16 inches (36–40 cm)
Color:	Yellowish-brown or gray
Location:	Southwestern United States, northern Central America, and South America
Roost:	Caves, mines
Food:	Nectar

Residents of the southwestern United States know all about the lesser long-nosed bat. If they're not careful, it will empty their hummingbird feeders at night! This bat, like most nectar feeders, can actually hover (remain in one place in the air) at a feeder while it drinks its dinner.

The main food of this desert dweller, however, is the nectar of cactus flowers. A long-nosed bat may visit as many as 100 flowers in a single night. It feeds by thrusting its pointy head and snout deep into the flower, then lapping up the nectar with its long tongue. By the end of the meal, the fur on the bat's face and neck will be covered with yellow pollen.

> It's amazing what you can see—when you really listen.

Chapter 3
Amazing Echolocation

You have already read that some bats use sound to "see" in the dark. This amazing ability is called *echolocation*.

Bats are not the only animals that use echolocation. Porpoises, shrews, and some types of whales, birds, and insects echolocate, too.

How Does Echolocation Work?

A bat sends out a steady stream of calls as it flies. It sends these calls from its mouth or nose. When these sounds hit an object, they bounce off it and return to the bat's ears in the form of echoes. The echoes are then "read" by the bat's brain and translated into images. This means that when the bat hears the echoes, its brain turns the echoes into a picture.

The Nose Knows

Some echolocating bats have odd-shaped noses, with lots of skin flaps and wrinkles. Scientists believe that these funny noses help the bat send its echolocation calls in the right direction.

Microbats also have a tragus, a small flap of skin in the ear. Scientists believe the tragus helps read the echoes.

Bats are incredibly good at this translation process. In fact, scientists believe bats probably get just as much information from sound as humans do from sight. Scientists have discovered that some bats can avoid obstacles as thin as a human hair in complete darkness. They can locate tiny prey crawling on the ground. They can even

The tragus, a flap of skin in a microbat's ear, helps the bat hear echoes.

The wrinkled skin on this microbat's nose is called a nose leaf.

tragus

nose leaf

pick their favorite bug out of a cloud of flying insects! Even when they aren't hunting, bats use echolocation to find their way in the dark.

returning echo

outgoing call

When a bat hears the returning echoes, its brain turns the echoes into a picture.

- The bat sends out a stream of loud, high-pitched calls. The calls travel away from the bat as sound waves.

- The sound waves bump into all the objects in a bat's flight path. The bumping does not happen all at the same time. A wave will bump into the closest part of an object just before it hits a part that is farther away.

- The sound waves "echo" back toward the bat. The bat's ears receive the echoes and send messages to the brain.

- The bat's brain then interprets the echoes in several ways. For example, it calculates how long the echo took to return. This amount of time tells the bat how far away the object is. The brain also notices tiny differences between the original calls and the echoes. These differences tell the bat about the object's shape and texture.

- The bat's brain puts all this information together to create a picture of the object.

All microbats echolocate. While some microbats send out echolocation calls through their noses and others send them through their mouths, all microbats use their vocal cords to produce echolocation calls.

> Bats that echolocate through the mouth are called oral emitters. They fly with their mouths open.

A few types of megabats produce echolocation calls by clicking their tongues. But most megabats don't use echolocation. They rely on their senses of sight and smell instead.

What Does It Sound Like?

A bat emits its calls in a series of short sounds. The number of calls depends on the situation. A bat calls slowly when it is just flying around. But when the bat locates prey, it will begin calling more rapidly. More calls create more echoes,

> The red bat normally sends out 10 echolocation calls per second. When it spots prey, it increases its calls to 200 per second!

which means the bat gets more information and has a better picture of its prey.

Most bat calls are *ultrasonic*, which means they are higher than the limits of human hearing. So we can't even hear them. To a bat, though, these calls may be deafening. Imagine a car horn blaring right in your ear. That's how loud some bat calls would be — if you could hear like a bat!

A device called a bat detector translates echolocation calls into sounds that humans can hear.

Do You Have to Shout?

Bats that feed in open spaces emit loud echolocation calls that travel far ahead of them. Loud bats are sometimes called "shouting" echolocators. The little brown bat is a shouter!

Bats that feed in forests and other cluttered areas are much quieter. They are sometimes called "whispering" echolocators. The common vampire bat is a whisperer.

On the Hunt

A bat uses echolocation to find prey, but it uses agility — quick, nimble moves — to catch it. Most bats, and especially the ones that eat flying insects, are acrobatic fliers. They can make a fast turn or take a dive to catch a bug. Sometimes they can

Bats' echolocation systems work billions of times better than the best human-built radar.

even take one "look" at a soaring insect, guess where it's going, and then intercept it with barely any maneuvering.

Bats that eat beetles, lizards, and other ground-dwelling creatures don't need to be quite as good at flying. Their echolocation skills, however, are just as amazing.

Whether the prey is in the air or on the ground, echolocation gives bats a big head start. Even "shortsighted" bats can locate prey from about 16 feet (4.9 m) away. And some types of bats can use echolocation to "see" as far as 50 feet (15.2 m)!

Bats make sounds other than their echolocation calls. Bats also squeak and squawk to communicate with one another.

The Drawbacks

Echolocation is a handy tool, but it doesn't guarantee a meal. Many kinds of animals can hear a bat's ultrasonic calls. Certain types of moths and praying mantises hide when they hear a bat coming. Some insects try to scare the bat away with loud noises or sudden movements. And other insects have discovered ways to communicate silently with one another by shaking leaves and twigs when a bat is in the area.

Some bats solve this problem by not making echolocation calls. Instead, these bats use their big ears to listen for the soft squeaks, croaks, or rustles made by their prey. Some bats can hear so well that they can locate bugs crawling across leaves just by listening!

But techniques like these are the exception, not the rule. Echolocation is the microbat's most important weapon in hunting. Without echolocation, bats would not be able to function in the dark — period.

Greater Bulldog Bat

• **Just the Facts** •

Suborder: Microchiroptera

Body: 4 inches (10.2 cm)

Wingspan: 22–28 inches (56–71 cm)

Color: Orange with a pale stripe down
              the back

Location: Central America and South America

Roost: Rocky crevices, caves, tunnels

Food: Fish

The greater bulldog bat uses echolocation as a fishing tool. It swoops low over ponds or other bodies of water and uses echolocation to scan the water's surface.

When the bat finds ripples made by small fish, it plunges its long, clawed feet into the water. The greater bulldog bat is very skilled at catching fish, which make up a big part of its diet.

Greater bulldog bats sometimes fall into the water by accident. But this is not a big problem. These bats are good swimmers. They can use their powerful wings to paddle themselves to dry land. Some individuals are even strong enough to take off straight from the water!

> We never slept like bats at my old school.

Chapter 4

Bats at Home

A bat's home is called its *roost*. Bats have three main types of roosts. They have day roosts where they take shelter in the daylight hours during the warm parts of the year. For females, the day roost is also a nursery roost where they raise babies. Bats also have hibernation roosts where they spend the winter. And they have temporary night roosts where they take breaks from hunting. Bats can have several night roosts that they go to on a regular basis.

The day roost is the home that most people picture when they think of bats.

Each evening, a bat leaves its day roost to search for food. And each morning, the bat returns to the same roost. It will spend most of the day hanging upside down and resting or rearing its young, saving its energy for another busy night of hunting.

Finding a Home

No matter where or how they roost, most bats have one thing in common. They choose their resting places for safety. There are many daytime

predators, including birds, snakes, dogs, cats, and even some insects, that would love to snack on sleeping bats. Hard-to-find or hard-to-reach roosts are a bat's way of making sure that this doesn't happen.

Bats also look for a roost that is the right temperature. This factor is very important to bats.

Just Hanging Around

- Bats that hang from the ceiling are safe from predators on the ground.
- Hanging by the feet helps a bat protect its delicate wings. It also leaves a bat's wings free, so it can wrap them around its body to keep warm while resting.
- Bats' bodies are well suited to the upside-down life. When a bat hangs, its toes "lock" into place. This keeps the bat from falling. Also, bats have special valves in their circulatory systems that keep blood from rushing to their heads as they hang.

Different Roosts

Many people think of caves when they think of bats. It is true that some types of bats do live in caves and abandoned mine shafts. These bats like being in darkness throughout the daytime hours. They also like the damp air in caves, which keeps their bodies from drying out.

Some bats would rather take shelter in hollow tree trunks. Others make their homes inside human-made structures such as attics and sheds. Some tropical bats crawl under broad leaves or other foliage. And some megabats, such as the

Pacific flying fox, simply hang in plain view from the upper branches of tall trees. They don't seem to need either privacy or darkness!

Pacific flying foxes may form treetop colonies of several thousand bats.

But this lifestyle isn't right for all bats. Many prefer to be tucked into a tight area to avoid predators. Some bats wedge themselves into cracks between rocks when daytime arrives. Others hide inside hollow bamboo stems or beneath loose tree bark. And some squeeze into gaps between boards, shingles, and other parts of buildings.

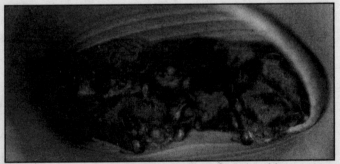

The most unusual bat roosts include animal burrows, flowers, large plant leaves, termite nests, and spiderwebs!

Bat Colonies

Most types of bats roost with other bats of their same species in groups called *colonies*. Some colonies contain just a few bats. But really big ones can contain millions of bats. These large bat colonies are usually found in caves and mine shafts. The bats hang from the ceiling, pressed tightly against one another like sardines in a can. In fact, colonies can be

How many bats did you say were in there?

so crowded that the bats have to crawl over one another if they want to move from one place to the next.

Although most bats roost in colonies, some prefer to be alone. Bats that roost by themselves are called solitary bats.

What a Mess!

When many bats live together, a lot of guano (bat droppings) piles up on the floor. The guano is 50 feet (15.2 m) deep in some parts of New Mexico's Carlsbad Caverns!

Bat guano is a great fertilizer. Lots of farmers use it on their crops. But it can also be dangerous to humans. Guano sometimes contains a fungus that can cause breathing problems if it is inhaled. So people should always wear a respirator or filter if they have to go near large quantities of bat guano.

As the world becomes more and more crowded with people, bats are having a harder time finding safe roosts. Areas that were forests just a few decades ago are now cities. Some caves that were

Eagle Creek Cave in Arizona was home to 30 million bats in the early 1900s. But the disturbance caused by tourists had reduced the colony to 30,000 by the 1960s.

once quiet and remote bat homes are now tourist spots that attract thousands of human visitors every year.

Many bats have grown used to humans. They have found new places to roost and they have adapted to living among people. But as bats' homes in the wilderness disappear, the bat population numbers are decreasing, too.

Each summer, more than a million bats take up residence beneath the Congress Avenue Bridge in Austin, Texas.

Little Brown Bat

• **Just the Facts** •

Suborder:	Microchiroptera
Body:	2 inches (5.1 cm)
Wingspan:	9–11 inches (22–27 cm)
Color:	Medium brown all over
Location:	United States and southern Canada
Roost:	Caves, buildings, trees
Food:	Beetles, moths, gnats, mosquitoes

Little brown bats are among the most common bats in the United States. They are also the bats most often found in human dwellings in the northern and eastern states. They thrive in high temperatures and will set up colonies in hot, dry attics whenever they can.

Little brown bats are very social. If one little brown bat finds a comfortable attic roost, hundreds or thousands may follow. This is good in one way: These bats can eat almost their entire weight in insects every night, so an attic colony can result in a bug-free home and yard. But a bat colony can be noisy and smelly, so some people don't like sharing their homes with little brown bats.

Tent-making Bat

• **Just the Facts** •

Suborder:	Microchiroptera
Body:	2.5 inches (6.4 cm)
Weight:	13–21 grams
Color:	Gray with a white stripe down the back and four white stripes on the face
Location:	Forest areas of Central America and South America
Roost:	Palm leaves
Food:	Mostly fruit, with some nectar and a few insects

Tent-making bats are named for their habit of creating "tents" from leaves. These little bats chew a row of holes in a leaf until the leaf weakens and folds toward the ground. Then they seek shelter underneath the drooping leaf. To hang upside down, they just stick their claws through the holes they chewed, then hang on tight.

Tent-making bats usually roost alone or in small groups. But 60 of these bats were once found in the tent of one single leaf!

Hey! Where did everyone go?

SEE YOU NEXT SUMMER!

Chapter 5

Migration and Hibernation

Bats thrive in warm weather. Why? To a bat, warmth means food. Fruit, flowers, insects, rodents, and other favorite bat meals are easy to find when temperatures are high.

But some bats live in areas that have distinct seasons, and the feast ends when winter approaches. Most bats that live in these areas feed on insects, and insects die in the cold weather. Therefore, the bats must find a way to get through the winter without starving.

Migrating Bats

Many bats solve this problem by heading to warmer climates for the winter. Then they will return to their summer home when the weather warms up again. This is called *migration*. Bats that migrate are *migratory*.

Unlike birds, migrating bats fly at night. This makes them very hard for scientists to track.

Some of the most common bats in North America are migratory. Mexican free-tailed bats, for example, form huge colonies in the southwestern United States during the summer, but they fly south to Mexico when winter approaches and their diet of flying insects disappears. Lesser long-nosed bats, which live on cactus flowers, migrate farther and farther south as the weather gets colder and the flowers in the northern part of the desert die off.

Some migrating bats fly as far as 1,000 miles (1,600 km) between their summer and winter homes. Others migrate just a few miles.

Hibernating Bats

Instead of migrating, other bats find a safe hiding place and sleep through the winter. This is called *hibernation*. Some types of bats hibernate in large groups. Others hibernate alone. In order to hibernate, bats start to store huge amounts of fat in the fall. The fat will be their only source of energy all winter.

Hibernacula

A place where any animal hibernates is called a hibernaculum. *Aculum* is a Latin suffix (word ending) that means "the place where something happens." So hibernaculum means the place where hibernation happens. The plural of hibernaculum is hibernacula.

Sometimes a hibernaculum can be very crowded.

Keeping Cool

A bat that is ready to hibernate finds a cold, damp, quiet place. (A cave where the air temperature hovers just above freezing is perfect.) The bat hangs upside down and closes its eyes. Then it does an amazing thing. Slowly, it lets itself get colder and colder until its body temperature is about the same as the surrounding air.

As the bat's temperature falls, its heart rate drops to 10–15 beats per minute or less. (While flying, a bat's heart may beat 1,300 times per minute!)

Its breathing and other bodily functions also slow down. This slowdown means that the bat uses much less energy than usual. A hibernating bat needs so little energy, in fact, that it can survive all winter by burning the fat it has packed onto its body during the autumn.

During hibernation, drops of dew often condense on a bat's fur.

Even during the summer, bats often enter a state or condition called *torpor*. Torpor is a lot like hibernation, but it is shorter and less extreme. In torpor, the bat's body cools down and slows down just a little bit. This lets the bat save a lot of energy during its daytime resting period.

Do Not Disturb

Bats burn 10 to 30 days' worth of energy each time they wake up from hibernation. A bat that is disturbed a few times during the winter burns so much energy that it will probably die 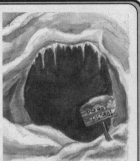 **before spring arrives. So it is very important not to disturb a hibernating bat!**

Heating Up

A bat that is waking up from either torpor or hibernation has to shiver to get warm again. Shivering raises the body's temperature through muscle activity. Every time a muscle moves, it creates a little bit of heat. Shivering

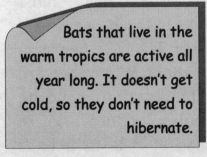
Bats that live in the warm tropics are active all year long. It doesn't get cold, so they don't need to hibernate.

requires thousands of tiny muscle twitches, so a sleepy bat quickly shakes itself warm and awake!

Shivering is an example of *thermoregulation,* which means controlling the body's temperature. Many mammals, including humans, automatically maintain a constant body temperature when they are healthy. But bats do not. Their temperatures go up and down all the time, depending on what they are doing or the temperature of their surroundings.

Some mammals sweat to release heat. But bats do not. A bat will sometimes lick itself to keep cool.

Because they have such a hard time keeping their bodies warm when they rest, most bats choose warm roosts in the summer. They let the warm air do the work for them. When they are hunting, bats have the opposite problem: Their bodies produce a lot of heat. But the blood vessels in a bat's wings act as a cooling system to help a bat to cool down. Bats will even fan their wings in an effort to stay cool.

Temperature is a big factor for bats, and their bodies have adapted special ways to deal with different levels of heat.

Eastern Pipistrelle

• **Just the Facts** •

Suborder:	Microchiroptera
Body:	1.65 inches (4.2 cm)
Wingspan:	8–10 inches (21–26 cm)
Color:	Yellowish-brown fur, reddish wings
Location:	Eastern United States and southern Canada
Roost:	Rocky crevices, caves, buildings, trees
Food:	Flying insects

Eastern pipistrelles are common throughout the eastern United States and southern Canada. During the summertime, these little bats roost mostly in rocky areas, buildings, and trees. But around October, they move into damp caves and prepare for a long winter of hibernation. During hibernation, their fur is often covered with tiny drops of dew from the moisture in the cave. While this is an amazing sight, beware of disturbing hibernating bats. It is against the law in many states and it jeopardizes the bats' chances of surviving the winter.

It's time for some baby talk!

Chapter 6
Bat Families

Summertime means more than just food to most bats. It also means babies.

Most female bats give birth to one baby every summer. The mother-to-be looks for a warm, humid roost. Most baby bats are born without fur, so heat is important. And damp air keeps the babies' delicate skin from getting too dry.

One at a Time

Most small mammals have litters, or groups of babies born at the same time. They may have several litters every year.

Most baby bats are born without fur, and their eyes are not yet open.

Bats, however, usually have just one baby, once a year. For their size, bats are among the slowest-reproducing animals in the world.

But they make up for this by living a long time. While many wild mice and other mammals that are about the same size as bats live just a year or so, bats can live longer than 30 years!

The Baby Is Born
Some species of bats hang upside down to have their babies. Others hold on with their thumbs and balance

themselves right side up. Right-side-up bats form a "basket" with their tail membranes to catch the baby as it is born.

Most newborn bats are hairless and helpless. Their wings are not fully developed, and their eyes are not ready to open. But a newborn bat instinctively knows what to do. It grasps its mother's fur with its claws and crawls up her body until it finds a

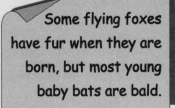
Some flying foxes have fur when they are born, but most young baby bats are bald.

nipple. Then it grabs the nipple with its strong baby teeth and holds on tight. It will drink its mother's milk through the nipple for several weeks.

Infant bats are huge compared to the newborns of other mammals. They may weigh a third as much as their mothers or even more! Imagine a human woman with a 40-pound (18.2-kg) newborn. That's what it would be like to be a bat mom.

Nursery Colonies

Some types of bats raise their babies all alone. Others form nursery colonies that may include millions of mothers and babies.

A big nursery colony is an incredible sight. During the daytime, mother-and-baby pairs are jammed into every crack and cranny. At night, when the mothers leave their babies to go hunting, the little bats move around on the ceiling of the roost. They squeak and crawl over one another until their mothers return.

It might seem as if it would be impossible for a mother bat to find her own baby

Most female bats raise their babies without any help from males.

among so many. But she can! A mother bat recognizes her baby's cries, and she also knows its smell. These clues help the mother to pick her baby out of the crowd.

All Grown Up

Baby bats grow up fast. In just a week their eyes open, their fur grows, and their wings become strong. By the time most baby bats are three to four weeks old, they are ready to fly on their own.

After a baby learns how to fly, it may go hunting with its mother a few times. But it quickly learns how to find its own food.

First Flight

Baby bats aren't good fliers at first. They sometimes fall to the ground. Once they are on the ground, they can't take off again. Scientists have seen baby bats crawling back to their roosts! A hard fall can injure a baby bat. Hurt babies are easy prey for snakes and other ground-dwelling predators.

The young bat remains in its nursery roost with its mother until all the bats leave for migration or hibernation. At this point, the baby bat is just a few months old, but it is already adult size. The next summer, the female bats will have their own babies.

A baby bat is sometimes called a pup.

Hoary Bat

• Just the Facts •

Suborder:	Microchiroptera
Body:	2.8 inches (7.2 cm)
Wingspan:	16 inches (40.6 cm)
Color:	Gray or brown, frosted with white
Location:	Southern Canada through South America; also Hawaii, Iceland, Bermuda, and the Dominican Republic
Roost:	The leaves of trees
Food:	Mostly moths

Most bats have just one baby at a time. But hoaries are different. They have two! A female hoary bat gives birth to one set of twins each spring. The mother stays with her babies during the daytime. But when night falls, she leaves the little bats hanging from twigs or leaves and flies off by herself to hunt.

Baby hoaries learn to fly when they are about one month old. The young bats stay close to their mother at first. Before long, though, they are big enough and strong enough to fly away and begin living on their own.

Psst!...Don't believe everything you hear about bats!

Chapter 7
Bat Myths

Many people have false beliefs about bats. For example, some people think bats will try to get into their hair. Others think that all bats carry diseases. Ideas like these cause many people to be afraid of bats.

So what are the myths, and what are the realities?

Myth #1: Bats Will Make a Nest in Human Hair.

This is not true! A human head would make an awful bat roost. There is no record of a bat ever getting caught in a person's hair. Bats do sometimes swoop low over people's heads. This may be the reason that people worry about their hair.

> If a bat gets trapped in your house, just open all the windows and doors. It will soon fly away.

But a swooping bat is probably just hunting. Lots of flying insects live around human dwellings, and bats must get close to humans if they want to catch these tasty bugs.

Myth #2: All Bats Carry Rabies.

Some people think that all bats carry rabies — a dangerous disease that is spread by animal bites.

This is not true. This myth actually

> Rabies is sometimes called *hydrophobia*, which means "fear of water." The disease got this nickname because rabies is a virus that can paralyze the throat muscles, so when rabid animals drink they look like they're choking.

came from scientists, who once believed that bats could carry and transmit this disease without getting sick themselves. But later studies proved this wrong. Today, we know that more than 99 percent of bats are healthy. In addition, you cannot catch rabies like you catch a cold — an infected animal has to bite you. So your chances of catching rabies from a bat are very small.

Still, you should never try to touch a bat. Any bat will bite in self-defense. You should see a doctor right away if a bat, or any wild animal, bites or scratches you.

Myth #3: Bats Are Blind.

There is an old expression, "blind as a bat." This saying comes from the common belief that all bats are blind. But they're not! As you have already

read, all bats can see, although some see better than others.

Bats even have an advantage over most animals. When conditions are bad for vision, they can use echolocation to "see." Between vision and hearing, a bat always has a lot of information about its surroundings.

Five Lucky Bats

In many parts of the world bats are actually symbols of good fortune. A Chinese symbol called the *wu-fu* represents good luck. The *wu-fu* symbol shows five bats surrounding a prosperity sign.

Myth #4: Vampire Bats Suck the
Blood Out of People!

Not true! Common vampire bats do
drink blood, but prey mainly on cattle
and other farm animals.
Each bat can only drink
about a spoonful of blood
before its belly is full.

The saliva of a
vampire bat contains
chemicals that stop
blood from clotting.

Common Vampire Bat

• Just the Facts •

Suborder:	Microchiroptera
Body:	3 inches (7.6 cm)
Wingspan:	15 inches (38.1 cm)
Color:	Grayish-brown
Location:	From northern Mexico to northern Argentina, Chile, and islands of the Caribbean
Roost:	Hollow trees, caves
Food:	Blood

Vampire bats are named after the legendary blood-sucking monsters because of their eating habits. Common vampire bats survive by drinking the blood of mammals, especially farm animals such as cattle and horses. There are very few reports of bats drinking blood from humans.

A vampire bat will land near its intended prey, then crawl closer. Most bats can't move quickly while on the ground, but the common vampire bat can crawl very well. When the bat reaches the prey, it nicks the skin with its two sharp front teeth. Blood flows, and the vampire bat laps it up with its grooved tongue. The process does not seem to hurt much. Most of the time, the vampire's prey doesn't even notice the vampire bat at all.

We owe bats a big thank-you.

CERTIFICATE OF APPRECIATION

Chapter 8

The Importance of Bats

Bats play very important roles in the natural world. Without bats, the number of insects would be out of control. Many of our favorite foods wouldn't exist. And forests would not grow. The more we know about bats, the more we can appreciate them.

Fewer Insects

Insect-eating bats reduce the number of bugs near their roosts. This is especially important in cooler climates, where the number of insects explodes during the spring and summer. A single bat can eat about 600 insects every hour. And it is estimated that the big Bracken Cave colony in Texas gobbles down 200 tons of bugs every night. Over the course of a summer, that's about 20,000 tons of insects eaten —by just *one* bat colony!

Bats eat many beetles and moths that like to munch on corn, wheat, and other agricultural products. Without bats, farmers would have to use a lot more pesticides to protect their crops from harmful insects.

A bat can eat about half its body weight in bugs each night.

Do you think I could eat half my body weight in chocolate?

Pollination and Reseeding

Bats that feed on fruit and flowers are also very important in the natural world. They help plants to reproduce through *pollination* (spreading pollen) and reseeding. When pollen from one flower gets into another flower, seeds are created. And seeds, of course, may eventually grow into new plants that produce flowers.

> Scientists can learn exactly what bats eat by studying their droppings.

A flower-feeding bat gets pollen all over its fur as it eats. Every time the bat feeds from a new flower, it leaves behind some of this substance. It also picks up some new pollen. A bat may visit hundreds of flowers in a single night, so it does a very good job of spreading pollen all over its territory.

> Some "bat-loving" flowers have special features to attract bats. They are pale in color so they can be seen in the dark and they open at night instead of during the day.

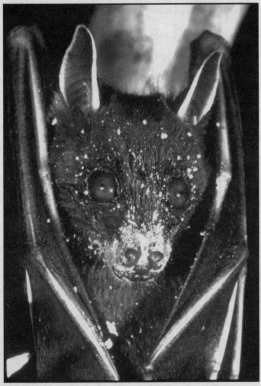

After a night of feeding, this bat's head and neck are covered with nectar.

Fruit-eating bats help by eating the seeds of different fruits. They spread these seeds all over their territories in their droppings. When the seeds land, they may take root and grow into new plants.

Many important crops depend on bats for pollination or reseeding. Here are just a few of the foods that come from plants that need bats to reproduce:

- Avocados
- Bananas
- Cashew nuts
- Cloves
- Dates
- Figs
- Mangoes
- Papayas
- Peaches
- And many more!

The seed-spreading function of bats is incredibly important. Scientists think that as much as 95 percent of all new rain-forest growth in the tropics starts from the seeds in bat droppings!

Some seeds need to be partly digested by a bat before they are able to sprout into a new plant.

Bat Protection

Unfortunately, some human activities are harmful to bats. New construction can destroy bat homes. Some common pesticides make bats sick or even kill them. And whole colonies of hibernating bats can die if human visitors interrupt their sleep. For these and other reasons, many bats are in danger of becoming extinct.

Conservationists — people who protect animals and natural resources — are working hard to keep this from happening. They are trying to teach people how to live with bats instead of destroying them. They are also creating new ways to protect bat colonies.

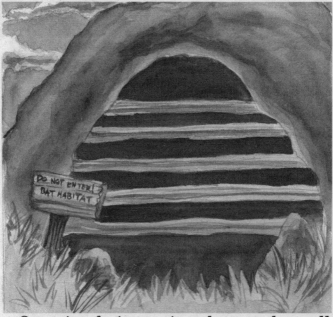

One simple invention that works well is the bat gate. To make bat gates, steel planks are welded across the mouths of caves. The slots between the planks are too small for a person to crawl through, but bats can get in and out without any trouble. A bat gate protects a colony without changing the bats' lifestyle.

Conservationists would also like people to put bat houses in their backyards. A bat house is a slender

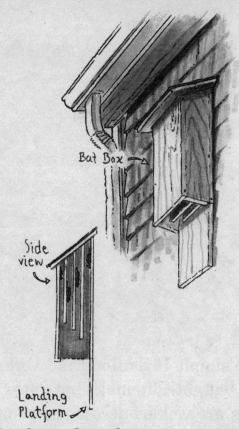

Bat Box →

Side view →

Landing Platform →

wooden box where bats can roost during the day. Bats like warm roosts, so it is important to place your bat house in a sunny place. It may take a couple of years for bats to discover a bat house. But once they do, the whole family may move in! Colonies of 200 to 300 bats are not uncommon.

There are advantages to having a bat colony close to your home: A yard never has any insect problems when bats are nearby!

What Can You Do?

You can put up a bat house to help the bat conservation effort. There are many organizations that can tell you how to build a bat house. You can even buy ready-made bat houses at many home and garden stores.

You could also sponsor a bat. (See "For More Info" on the following page for the addresses of organizations with bat sponsorship programs.) These programs send you a certificate, stickers, and pictures of your bat in return for a small donation.

For More Info

Bat Conservation International (BCI) is the oldest and largest bat-related organization in the United States. BCI provides information about bats and supports conservation and research projects. It also publishes Bats *magazine. BCI can help you to sponsor a bat, build a bat house, find books about bats, and much more!*

You can write to BCI at P.O. Box 162603, Austin, TX 78716. You can also visit them on the Internet at www.batcon.org

Here are some other cool Web sites:

Bat World Sanctuary — This organization helps injured bats.

www.batworld.org

Discovery Channel's Bat Cam — See live bats at the National Zoo in Washington, D.C.!

www.discovery.com/cams/bat/batmain.html

The most important thing you can do, however, is spread the word about bats. Now that you have read this book, you understand how interesting and important these creatures are. You can make a big difference just by telling people what you have learned!

Real Bats
Samoan Flying Fox

• Just the Facts •

Suborder:	Megachiroptera
Wingspan:	6 feet (about 2 m)
Color:	Dark brown
Location:	Samoa
Roost:	Tree branches
Food:	Fruit, flowers, nectar

The Samoan flying fox is found only on the South Pacific island of Samoa. With an average wingspan of 6 feet (about 2 m), it is one of the biggest bats in the world.

This flying fox has some unusual habits. For one thing, it feeds during the daytime. Its big wings also allow it to soar like an eagle. Most bats have to flap when they fly to stay in the air.

Unfortunately, the Samoan flying fox is in danger of extinction. Logging operations have destroyed much of the bat's habitat. This animal is also hunted for food. The Samoan government has put limits on bat hunting — but these efforts may not be enough to save this magnificent creature.

INDEX